RED PROMISES

To Mr. Craig for
as a bribe for
a residency in
the lovely manse
(so I can find the peacock to
the wood to
my heart's content)

Love
Halli

ESSENTIAL POETS SERIES 105

Guernica Editions Inc. acknowledges the support of
The Canada Council for the Arts.
Guernica Editions Inc. acknowledges the support of the Ontario Arts Council.
Guernica Editions Inc. acknowledges the financial support of the Government of Canada
through the Book Publishing Industry Development Program (BPIDP).

HALLI VILLEGAS

H. Villey

RED PROMISES

GUERNICA
TORONTO·BUFFALO·LANCASTER (U.K.)
2001

Copyright © 2001, by Halli Villegas and Guernica Editions Inc.
All rights reserved. The use of any part of this publication, reproduced, transmitted in
any form or by any means, electronic, mechanical, photocopying, recording or otherwise
stored in a retrieval system, without the prior consent of the publisher is an infringement
of the copyright law.

Antonio D'Alfonso, editor
Guernica Editions Inc.
P.O. Box 117, Station P, Toronto (ON), Canada M5S 2S6
2250 Military Road, Tonawanda, N.Y. 14150-6000 U.S.A.
Gazelle, Falcon House, Queen Square, Lancaster LA1 1RN U.K.

Typeset by Selina.
Printed in Canada.
First edition.

Legal Deposit – First Quarter
National Library of Canada
Library of Congress Catalog Card Number: 2001116530

National Library of Canada Cataloguing in Publication Data
Villegas, Halli
Red promises
(Essential poets series ; 105)
ISBN 1-55071-130-X
I. Title. II. Series.
PS8593.I3894R43 2001   C811'.16   C2001-900190-8
PR9199.3.V488R43 2001

Contents

Acknowledgements 6
Pear Tree 9
Feuillton 10
Devil's Advocate 12
Minor Miracles 13
Social Services 15
The Pailleron Children, 1881 17
Bloom 18
Marie Claire 19
The Doll House 20
I Used to Want to be a Nun 22
Regrets 24
Clipped Wings 25
Capote 26
Oedipus Not 27
Cone at King and Bay 29
Change in the Weather 31
A Trifle of Hearts 33
I've Waited All Week 34
Personal Mythology 36
Madame X 38
Cherry 39
Red Ribbon 40
One White Violet 42
Three Deer 43
Cantus 45
R.R. 47
Strawberries and Weeds 50
Cassandra 51
In the City, Woman, Man 56
Painter 57
The Snare 60
Winter Wardrobe 61
I Worry Where I Will Be Buried 62

Acknowledgements

A special thank you to Dr. Bruce Meyer, without whom this book would never have even been conceived, let alone realized. Thank you also to Dr. Austin Clarke, and to my editor, Antonio D'Alfonso whose advice and encouragement was invaluble. Thank you to all my friends for their support, especially Julie Roorda, Robin Blackburn, Sue Bowness, Colin Carberry and John Stiles. Thanks to all the Pagiticats and *Pagitica* in Toronto for giving me my big break into the world of literary magazines. Thanks to Stephanie Bolster for her suggestions and insights into some of these poems. Finally thank you to my family in Detroit, including Jo Hicks, who provided the inspiration and the foundation for all of the poems. Love you all.

References: "Madame X": Painting by John Singer Sargent, 1884; "The Pailleron Children, 1889": Painting by John Singer Sargent, 1889 ; "Miss Otis Regrets": Cole Porter; "A Trifle of Hearts": "Lush Life" by Billy Strayhorn; "I've Waited All Week" was inspired by the Tom Waits song "Tango Till They're Sore."

For Misha, David and Paul

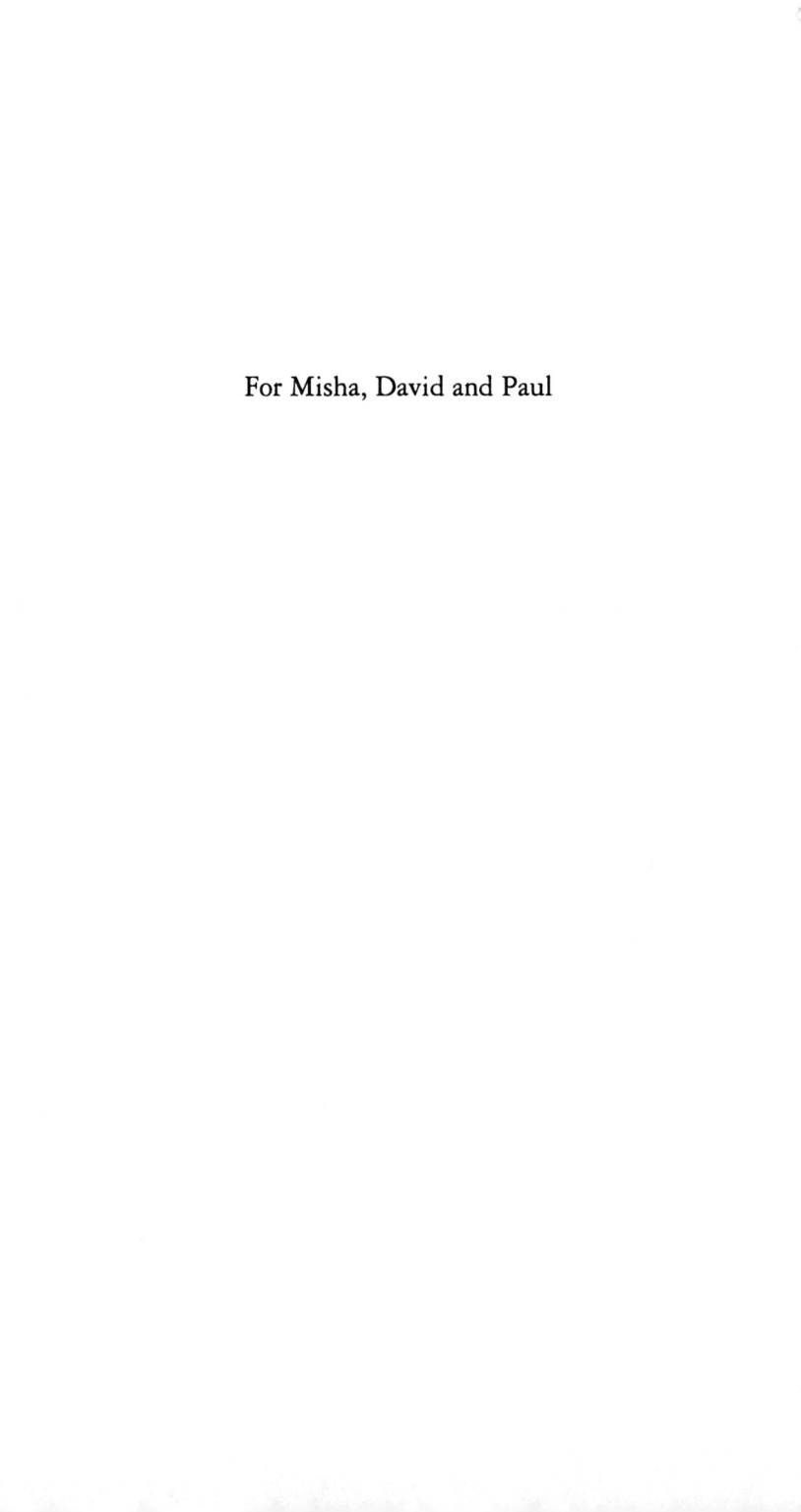

Pear Tree

Sickly sweet, gone over.
Can't you smell it?
It's the pear tree in the yard.

This house – full already of late heat
and early cold –
is topped off now with its heavy scent.

Fallen from our
reasonable stance
into attitudes of blame

frustrated by the sheer stupidity
of forgetting this inevitable end
to a fecund season

we berate each other
for not (as we had sworn to do last year)
raking up the fruit

before
it had a chance to rot

Feuillton

At sixteen
told to empty out a closet
no one had used for years
I dislodged
a pile of photos.

I raked them up off the carpet with my hands
flipped over the first,
saw:
wedding pictures,
my mother and her bridesmaids,
my mother in front of the church, my mother
with some white man in a tuxedo she smiles as they
cut a three tiered cake
hands jointly clasped
over the knife handle.

Who's that guy?
"That was my first husband."
Why did you divorce him?

My mother turned her head
looked at me from the corners of her eyes
said:
"I was bored of being married."
Then she turned to face me full on,
asked me if I was finished.

That same summer I had to clean the garage.

In a back corner where last fall's leaves had been left untouched
I found a glossy brown suitcase,
with green corroded locks.
Inside, my mother's first wedding dress.

Half rotted already,
when I dragged it into the sunlight
it disintegrated,
flakes of lace
fell from my fingers
landed on the grass:
a hundred yellowed leaves.

Devil's Advocate

Was her childhood really relentlessly bad?
Didn't she secretly like sometimes
the bird's eye view being different had
given her of other's lives?

And wasn't she just a little proud
of her collapsed defiant home
in a picture perfect neighbourhood
that left her to herself alone?

From this past she chooses the sacrifice
to placate an angry god, her heart.
Would a happy childhood still suffice
for her unsentimental art?

Isn't she pleased things worked out this way?
I think she is, though she might never say.

Minor Miracles

We were the house that stones fell on
one hot suburban summer afternoon.
They rained down from the empty
atmosphere as children rode their bikes
past and a Golden Retriever endlessly retrieved a red ball
thrown by a man in plaid bermudas whose wife

knelt in her garden and chatted with the wife
of the man who had mowed his lawn twice already on
that warm summer weekend. The dog's wet ball
spun one last time through the afternoon
air, before landing beside abandoned bikes
whose owners stared at the now empty

sky above our house with faces empty
of expression. One neighbour called his wife
out to see, but the children picked up their bikes
and went to get ice cream from the store on
the corner. The break in the afternoon
caused by the stones ended. Dog found his ball

and master threw ball
arching it towards the dog's mouth, waiting eager and empty.
It was another ordinary summer afternoon
when the Virgin Mary (yes, His wife)
appeared in our garage traced clearly in rust on
the old Toyota which stood surrounded by broken bikes,
spokeless ghosts of summers past. Among these bikes

tumbled like petitioners at Lourdes, the virgin gazed at a deflated ball
left in a corner, her mournful eyes turned as always on
the forsaken. Pilgrims came in a steady stream and never with empty
hands. They brought flowers, votive candles; one man brought his wife
to pray for their gangster son's soul all afternoon.

Our neighbours never came. Instead, the next afternoon
they called the police. Claimed their children's bikes
had gone missing, and that the crowds kept every wife
from feeling safe. The dog was kept in, but his rubber ball
left behind in the grass nearly tripped the cop who came to empty
out the strangers and set the switch of daily life back to on.

By the end of the afternoon the street was empty, the ball confiscated.
Bikes that had been lost, miraculously found on porches and in garages.
All was in order,
and taking a stone from our lawn, that man and his wife went to pray
somewhere else.

Social Services

Once after the divorce
our old dryer broke down.
My mother's only course
was to string the laundry
on a line across the enclosed porch
that ran the front of our house.

It was raining, you see,
and we needed clean tights for school.
Figured what trouble would there be
from drying laundry on a line
hidden by our porch's screens
while my sister and I played

in the wet front yard
gathering dandelions to match our slickers.
We were startled by the strange car
that pulled into our drive. A man with a clipboard
got out, asked to see our mother. We stared hard
at him. I broke first, ran and called her from the house.

She came out, greeted the man
They stood in the drizzle talking.
He asked her how long did she plan
to leave the laundry strung on the porch?
The neighbours had complained, did she understand?
Sent Social Services down. This was not after all Appalachia.

My mother started to cry
told him the dryer was broken, it had been raining all day.
I hated her then and didn't know why.
The man seemed to relent said take the clothes
down. Mother nodded relieved and shy.
At nine I saw how young she was.

She went into the house to do as he said
and he got in the car and left.
My sister and I stood in the rain filled with the dread
of knowing the eyes of the street were upon us.
That day I saw how young she was
I wished something would strike the neighbours dead.

The Pailleron Children, 1881

In the dark of the drawing room they play
games that have no end. Her white dress a gleam
against blood red draperies and the sheen
of mahogany. Is it night or day
when the painter comes? Interrupts their way
of making hours pass in this heavy
household. Opens curtains to let in a beam
of light. Places the children, makes them stay
still. They hate the eye that observes closely
pins them down. Butterflies on a spreading
board for the pleasure of their parents whim.
Edouard leans, whispers to Marie-Louise.
They cannot have your soul or anything
you do not let them have. Don't let them in,
or else, the grownups win.
She loves her brother better than herself
guardian of their childhood's secret wealth
she is six, he is twelve.
They will close the drapes when the painter's done,
and shield themselves from the adult's sun.

Bloom

Raised in my father's garden, I am his prize possession.
Each day among belladonna, mistletoe, nightshade,
I walk in my dress of seed pearls and brocade,
whisper to the marble statues my confession,
I am not happy in this world my father made.

Rooted here I cannot breathe outside
this place. Poison blooms from my lips
scents my skin. I've never heard another voice
or seen another soul. Only father speaks to me

from behind a wooden wall. Perhaps I have a choice
and this is just a dream. I've never really tried
to leave, I've taken father's word.
A real father would not doom his child,
perhaps my dream father has lied.

Could it be the voice I've heard
was inside me all the while?

Marie Claire

A fuller sexier bustline.
Chanel bag in the palest lime
green and in between:
A woman unseen.
Veiled, hidden there behind

imprisoning folds. Square of mesh
to view the world. No inch of flesh
to tempt the weaker
male deep into her
sinful trap. She's a test

of power, of control that men
in her country won't fail again.
Mutilated, stoned
daily torture honed
until she can't pretend

that she is better off alive.
She is there waiting next to *Five
Ways to Please Your Mate*
and *Your First Blind Date:
We Can Help You Survive.*

The Doll House

Father reads the paper
propped on the couch.
His china head
glistens with black hair
painted to form a deep widow's peak.
A thin moustache attempts
to make masculine
the cupid bow mouth.

Mother's blue paint slash eyes
stare fixedly at the *papier maché* ham
placed on the dining room table.
She stands leaning over the table
in a pink cotton dress
that echoes the ham's inedible
lacquered flesh.

In bed mother and father's china heads
make any arrangement of passion
impossible.
The maid has a chipped nose
from an earlier experiment.

Up in the nursery
brother rides a rocking horse.
He cannot quite be made to sit upright,
he faces the floor.
Useless, his red boots

and plump white china calves
dangle at the horse's sides.

Sister stares at herself
in her bedroom mirror.
Moulded to be permanently
on the threshold of womanhood,
she wears a blue satin dress
that won't come off.

The doll house forms their universe:
one tableau after another
in a stiff parody. Moved through their rooms
by outside forces.
To play parts
they have no say in imagining.

I Used to Want to be a Nun

Empty house after school
I run to my room, strip,
and read naked on my bed.
Or maybe I stand
in the middle of the dining room
and sing every show tune I know
at the top of my voice.

Then I collapse
face forward onto the floor,
arms outstretched, palms down
feet overlapped
like a novitiate.
With my ear pressed to the carpet
I listen to the house.

It whispers
constant proximity does not equal
love.
Says to me
although it seems to shelter us
it is indifferent to our rattles
through its rooms.

I lie there until
over the voice of this dwelling place
I hear my heartbeat,
the rhythmic sluice of my blood
through my body.

Regrets

Miss Otis regrets she's unable to lunch today, madam.
She had one too many ice cold, lethal martinis last night.
Played over and over, an old Billie Holiday album.
That indigo music shot through with violet, back alley light.

She had one too many ice cold lethal martinis last night.
Thought she would banish the blues with slow jazz and booze,
    listen to
that indigo music shot through with violet, back alley light;
and try to remember just what it was she once saw in you.

Thought she would banish the blues with slow jazz and booze.
    Listen to
a voice that could distill plain heartache into something sublime
and try to remember just what it was she once saw in you.
Her dream of love had flown, so last evening she needed to find

a voice that could distill plain heartache into something sublime.
Now in the morning she must face what she would like to forget.
Her dream of love had flown, so last evening she needed to find
solace of some sort, a way to end the unending regret.

Played over and over, an old Billie Holiday album,
Miss Otis regrets she's unable to lunch today, madam.

Clipped Wings

They peck along the paths
beneath the cities
economic redwoods.

Thin women in black,
hair indiscriminate
between blond and brown.
Neat lipstick, careful good looks,

unruffled, no hint
of the roseate aureole
or pearled thigh
under city suited feathers.

What their money will buy:

Clean lined clothes
hung in a house done in beige.
A cell-phone husband
with a steady income of his own.

They chatter like doves disturbed.

This is important.
This is life, they say.
Never will they catch your eye.
Bird glance, bounce away.

Capote

Pinned to a line a red dress hangs there
above the monochromatic incurious crowd;
it snaps in the wind, an unspoken dare.

In this arena, angular, spare,
where shadows form an endless shroud,
pinned to a line a red dress hangs there.

A high wire act suspended mid air
between buildings that are stone cold and proud,
it snaps in the wind, an unspoken dare.

People pass beneath it to offices where
the rules are in stone and no living allowed.
Pinned to a line a red dress hangs there

and once in a while someone stops to stare,
then he hurries along with his head bowed.
It snaps in the wind, an unspoken dare

for those who may have hidden somewhere
a discontent never spoken aloud.
Pinned to a line a red dress hangs there.

In this life nothing is fair.
Death is the picador goading us on and
pinned to a line a red dress hangs there.
It snaps in the wind, an unspoken dare.

Oedipus Not

In that office building a little to the left
whose windows reproduce in an abstract way
the building opposite,
there each day

is the man who loves his mother.

He doesn't live at home, moved out
ten years ago. He's not a horn rimmed geek
who mends his glasses at the bridge
with masking tape, this is a Greek

tragedy. He's been married,
happily at times, for six and a half years.
The sight of his wife as she
held their newborn son brought tears

to his eyes along with a firm resolve to be
as good a dad as daddy had
always been. Remembering camping trips
with papa as a lad

bring to mind a photo of his mother
he had chanced to discover,
stuck in the old dresser he had taken
from home for the other

bedroom in his house. The picture was shot

in his mother's maidenhood. She stood beside a tent
wearing harlequin glasses, a swirled brown bang.
He wondered briefly where those glasses went,

then looked closer at her unmarried face,
realized with a thrill that he could see
her future, all the girl in the photo
does not know of what is yet to be.

The plaid shirt, dungarees,
the red-lipsticked mouth and shiny hair.
In her eyes and her tan legs,
his entire life is embryonic there.
This sums up the wonder of his mother
that he felt from the first:
he is in her as she is in he.

In his mirrored offices this man
keeps a staff of three young women. They look
alike: Brown hair, bangs and glasses
in the latest style. It took

us just a moment to see, it really is uncanny,
but he would call you crazy
if you pointed out the triplicate of mama
on that camping trip one hazy

summer, forty-five years past,
he has managed to achieve
there
in his office tower of glass.

Cone at King and Bay

Even if you are dressed conservatively
eating an ice cream cone at King and Bay
will attract the attention of men in suits.

Better if it is pink and you lick
slowly along the rim and don't
look at the men at all.

It will remind them of so many things
but especially
what they have covered
with Hugo Boss tropical weight wool
and Calvin Klein cotton.

The phalanx of blue and grey
will break into faces,
briefly something
besides economics
in their eyes.

Suck the ice cream to a point
and lick it flat again.
Walk away.
Towards Queen or Yonge or Union Station,
anywhere, don't look back.

It is enough to know you have left them
a little less satisfied with themselves,
with their designer clothes
a bit
tight in the crotch.

That is the power
of an ice cream cone
at King and Bay.

Change in the Weather

Square of green pinned down
by the cement of the city.
People prone on its surface,
prick of the grass,
a bed of nails.

Women push up their skirts,
expose winter white thighs.
Men loosen collars noosed by ties.
All close their eyes, pretend
a lunch hour is a life.

She passes the park in a suit
too dark and heavy for the hot day
a red carnation wilts in a buttonhole
a run in the left leg of her black stockings,
stops at the corner where a man

carves sphinxes from bars of Ivory Soap.
She puts a dollar in his cup,
picks a sphinx from the row
ranged on an empty fax paper box.
It smells sweet, solid in her hand.

He doesn't look up,
flakes fly from beneath his knife
as he creates
another mystery.
Behind her
sweat trickles down
the women's thighs
snakes under the men's collars
but where she stands
snow flies.

A Trifle of Hearts

In his voice it is always the old night.
Even across telephone lines, the low
flat note of twelve o'clock tales. I won't go.
I've emerged from the yellow light
of places I've listened in to the bright
early street where morning is falling slow
petals from a blue blossom. The last show
is done. Still, I remember being tight
and with drunken ease telling him I heard
his sound with my soul. Ah yes, of course,
I was wrong. He didn't want to be known.

Instead he played at being Rollins or Bird,
tried to shirk the self that clung with such force.
Picked their music clean down to the bone;
nothing there of his own.
Now I let the machine pick up his call,
and when his tired out riffs begin to fall,
I can just delete them all.
Nothing there I need to hear any more.
Same song again, could only be a bore.

I've Waited All Week

I want to hang out of the window with confetti in my hair,
drink too much, dance close to you until we both feel like
    falling down.
Sheer black stockings with a seam up the back and a red dress to
    wear,
that's all I need tonight. You call the taxi to take us downtown.

In the taxi when I run my hand across the front of your brown
neatly pressed pants, I know you will touch my breasts and
    quietly swear.
Ask the driver to turn up the music while we're fooling around.
I want to hang out of the window with confetti in my hair.

The city's lights are like leftover stars pasted any old where.
People's voices, sirens and the streetcar mingle to form a sound
that echoes the thrill when I look over and see you there.
Drink too much, dance close to you until we both feel like
    falling down

is my plan for the evening. Right now I feel so tightly wound
I need to stop here in the street to kiss, again, again on the stair.
All day I wanted you, so I went out shopping and found
sheer black stockings with a seam up the back and a red dress to
    wear.

Eyes closed, hips touching, we've danced like lover's having their first affair,
we clung so close your sweat soaked through the front of my brand new red gown.
Kissed on the dance floor while others were watching and just didn't care.
That's all I need tonight. You call the taxi to take us downtown

for one last drink before calling it quits. Then we'll start homeward bound
and in the taxi dark I will taste you drying on my skin. Blare on city, I am lost in my lover's mouth and in silence drown.
Roll down the glass to catch the last breath of this night's passion drunk air.
I want to hang out of the window.

Personal Mythology

My stiff halo of lust,
red with singed edges,
fits me,
makes me a saint of sorts.

My mark,
a sign that brings out
the slit eyes, stiff lips of jealousy.

People stop to stare at the flames
that sprout
shoot
from the top of my head.
They pick their way gingerly
among the sparks
that fall from my lips
when I speak.

In their eyes
I see the reflection.
Tiny fires
echo my own.

Don't speak to me of sin.
Like the three fates
who spin life, weave death,
this is what I feel
tumble from my hands.

Power to create
power to end just as abruptly
with the click clack of silver shears
shaped like a swan
ravishing the unsuspecting.

Madame X

The weight of her dress's jewelled strap
slipped off her shoulder, reminds her
of her power. The simple fact

that its position caused a stir
tells of the disturbance she can
arouse, the unsettling allure

of studied artifice. Her fan
is used to play up dark-rimmed eyes
set beneath brows whose perfect span

has been chosen and realized
by her own steady hand before
a gilt mirror. She buys

lavender-coloured powder for
enhancing the opalescent
sheen of her skin. Despise or

admire these tricks that are meant
to bring into focus what is seen –
she turns your head. Maybe then

you imagine her in between
your sheets in an unstudied scene.
It's your hand that reaches out to trap
the solid weight of her dress's jewelled strap.

Cherry

First one picked from the bowl
held up to the light for the pleasure
of its clouded garnet hanging from your fingers.
Flushed skin yields beneath your teeth
and the whole is tasted.
In the centre, a secret
polished in your mouth
pushed out through stained lips
into your palm.
To finish
tie a knot in the stem
with your tongue.
Lay it glistening on the rim of a plate.

Red Ribbon

There is a red ribbon
woven into the nest
robins have made in the corner
of our porch
where the gingerbreading
forms a shelf.

I know that ribbon.
I wore it to hold the hair off my face
the first warm day
this spring
when we took a blanket
to a grassy spot
down by the creek.

While you talked
I pulled the ribbon from my hair
smoothed it across my thigh,
felt the silk and turned edge
against my skin
as I listened.

Then when I spoke
I wound it round my wrist,
the red bright on pale flesh
with lacy turquoise veins
running under it.

Finally there were no more words.
I loosed the ribbon into the grass,
saw the sky once:
blue soon hidden
by your face.

The robins have the ribbon.
Among the utilitarian art
of their twigs it gleams.
We have been together
four years now.

When you are next to me
and there are no more words
between us,
cherry red ribbons
still fall
from my hands.

One White Violet

Be blunt, be plain.
Understand the nuance of gesture
open or protective,
across the body, in the face.

Know how the interlace of trees
outside a dirty window
will change with the seasons
and a good cleaning of the glass.

Hang a saffron curtain.
Wash the blue willow bowl.
In water pearled with soap
see the figures start to move
across the bridge. Two birds
swoop and soar as the story unfolds.

Note my lover's footprint in the snow.
Fills with slush,
melts away into the earth, sprouts
one white violet.

Three Deer

When I was young
in the white silence of winter I saw a deer
hung to drain from a tree branch.
On the pristine snow beneath its inverted carcass
was a Rorshach of blood.
Rose or skull
I couldn't decide.

The deer's velvety muzzle and
half lidded eye looked resigned
to its suspended state
there in the crooked tree at the edge
of a grey roiling lake.

Older on the way to work in the greening spring,
new to this countryside,
intent on finches, foxes
even the occasional coyote,
I saw a deer
dead alongside the tarmac.

The deer's thin neck arched back
split with a red gash.
The narrow muzzle, closed eyes
seemed to accede to its supine position
on the side of an asphalt river
with rolling wheels in waves.

The other day
on the way home in summer heat's insistent pressure
something flashed into the weeds along the road.
My first thought was the neighbours' dog
off its leash.

As I came upon the place
where the grasses had parted and closed so quickly
I saw a deer.

Immobilized, I stood,
looked at that deer
while he, defiant and whole,
across a sea of still yellow stalks
eyed me wide open.

Cantus

Shag wolves gather in the north field.

They come through the bush,
cross the creek.
Water twists the hair on their bellies
into crystal tipped teats
that sway with the rhythm
of their lope.

Up through paths
which even during the day
have dark secret places
where the earth's breath is cooler
and starflowers appear
radiant
upon the black mat of decay.

The shag wolves' high curled cries
scale the night to hang
constellations of sound
in the frost laden sky.

When their song is hung
as the season demands,
they are impelled onward

the way that the stars
wheel through successive skies
and fade away at dawn.

R.R.

I can see her

in a white frame house set far back from the road.
Take the stone path past the apple tree
that shades the porch.
Cookers those apples
good for pies or preserves.

Up the broad front steps into the house.
Seldom used parlour on your right,
painted eyes of family on the mantelpiece
watchful over the ruby plush,
dust motes suspended in the lace filtered
afternoon sun.

Go back,

back to the heart of the house, to the kitchen.
In an apron, hair tidy, she peels apples for a pie.
Festive curls appear beneath the knife
as her hands move in rhythm with the clock.
Cat in the rocker stretches as the men,
hungry now in the fading sun,
head across the fields towards the house.

She falls to the kitchen floor, a tumbled doll.
Her dress disarranged, exposes the white underclothes
she had carefully bleached

and hung to dry in the long sun.
The table is overturned. Apples
roll to the darkest corners, red stains
on her clean floor.

She's not dead.
Just dead tired.

Only needs to close her eyes and the clock will stop
long enough to let her catch her breath. The men
will freeze in the fields until she has time to think;
all the days will wait for her to choose her life.

She has loosed her hold,
red-winged angels and demons crowd in, lift her up
carry her away.

As they pass
their feathers leave unsightly streaks
along the doorjambs, but it is none of her concern now.

She rises.
Rises with them into the flat blue sky.
We lose sight of her

though we shade our eyes to search for her figure.
In the blank sky unseen she
has settled at the top of the apple tree.
Her hair is tangled among the boughs.
Her long wings glossy feathers are mistaken for leaves,
each of her branches

twisted by their search for sun
are tipped with red round droplets.

Strawberries and Weeds

Near the field there is a strawberry patch
smothered with weeds that almost bar your way
with rough haired leaves and dry hooks that catch
on any bit of foolish flesh. Today,
the fruit gleams under these barbed guardians.
Red promises nearly obscured by last
years neglect. But if you gauntlet your hands
with canvas gloves and start to pull the past
from the ground, roots and all, you can clear a
place to squat, then reach under the leaves of
the plants. Tug the berry gently, the way
you would reach your hand out to one you love.
Eat the first one sitting among the weeds.
Follow wherever that strawberry leads.

Cassandra

1

I
stand in front of my pier glass
and talk to myself
so I know that someone listens.
She, me looks back,
mimics the gesture with which
I pull my sodden red hair
into a knot at my nape.

2

See
this dress simply hangs on me.
I am insubstantial in it,
bones and flesh strung together
with wide eyed energy.
Merino wool, Italian tailoring,
even a Gucci heel
cannot hide the fact
that I am dwindling.

3

I
cross my legs.
The rasp of my sheer black stockings
attracts the notice of the man
across from me.

He
lowers his paper slightly
his glance becomes longer,
travels the length of my leg,
stops at the shadow
beneath my skirt.

I look at the window.
The rain is like quicksilver
on the glass.

4

My office is quiet,
save for the death watch beetle;
my secretary, typing.

We
dislike each other cordially.
She never listens,
I suspect she covets my position.
She thinks I patronise her.

Soon the phone will ring
and she will pass the call
to me.

My voice
disembodied from myself
will speak into it like an oracle.

5

In business
I know when to buy or sell.
They
can't quite believe my pretty mouth
has made them so much money.

Over the phone its fine
but when they meet me
its dinner and drinks
and let's not talk business
and finally
let's not talk
at all.

6

This bar was a mistake.
Even in dim light
I cannot loose clear sight.

Three men have bought me drinks
and left as quickly as they came.

My mother taught me
what a man likes to hear.
I mean to say those things
but to my horror
I tell the truth.

Now they stare at me
as if I
had asked them to do something
unnatural.

7

(The three men speak)
Jesus, she's good looking,
but so damn depressing,
a real downer.
We could have had fun
if she hadn't said a word.

A five dollar drink
to hear that —
Who does she think she is?
I don't even let my wife
talk to me like that.

I thought she looked lonely,
thought a drink would cheer her up.
You never can tell,
I guess I read her wrong.
She was obviously waiting for someone.

8

The city falls behind me.

We
ride this train packed knee to knee.

As if it will never end,
they sleep.
Heads slump, papers slip
from released grips.
So many lives
depend upon illusion.

The sun through the window
touches each face
before its gone for good.

They
sleep on.
Lulled by the monotonous rock
of this ride.

9

At home, unable to sleep
I lie flattened
beneath the sheet moonlight
carves like marble,
I pray
for someone to have pity.

Cloud my inner eye.
Stop
my mouth.

In the City, Woman, Man

Smoke of her red lips
black rim of her mascara
smeared by the late hour.

Her breasts like bullets.
A gun ready to go off
beneath her leather jacket.

The metallic tang
of liquor on her tongue when
she tastes her fresh drink.

He plays the market.
Slips his wedding band into
his waiting pocket.

Watches her over
the rim of his whiskey glass.
A long slow swallow.

Ice cube held in his mouth,
he bites down. Shatters what
was ready to melt.

The city is indifferent.
They never thought otherwise.

Painter

When the sun had just begun to tint the sky,
we started along the path to the river.
Carried the tools of our trade
canvas, paints,
small easels and stools.
Some smoked, others judged the quality of light,
squinted their eyes, tilted their heads
side to side.

I whistled softly
a café tune that had run through my head
since morning.

Our model walked among us.
She ate from a handful of cherries
aimed the stones at our hats.
When we reached the river she shed her robe.
After some discussion
we arranged her against a tree;
the water behind her,
a blue veil caught by wind.

As I painted water, grass,
her breasts and solid haunch,
I was reminded of my mistress
who never liked the models much
though she once was one herself.
It seemed to me they should be sisters,

having shared the same position.

*This model
with the sky of ecclesiastical blue behind her
could be a Madonna.
I should paint her with angels that hover near
while seraphim whisper in her ear
of miracles, great blessings —
that will not be unmixed.*

But as that style is out of date
I let the vision pass.

At lunch we talked of art and beauty
till all that was left
were three empty bottles of Burgundy
and bits of lamb stuck to the willow platter.
One by one the others fell asleep,
scattered in the grass like toppled reliquary.
One slept with his head in our model's lap
while she smoked quietly, stroked his hair
from time to time.

I left them,
meaning to escape indolence
with a row up the river in the boat
moored beneath the willows.
Once there
I only laid my head down
for a minute.

Light shifted through the trees
The heat, the sway
must have lulled me to sleep.

Later it seemed I heard a women call.
Her voice searched for me
in the deepening twilight.
I could not tell if it was my model
or my mistress.

For a moment my vision by the river
hung before me.
I didn't answer the call.

Instead
I closed my eyes
and slept on.

The Snare

Thin wire cuts across the neck.
Ruff of fur clotted with blood
head thrown back, eyes at half mast;
death's milky cast. In the mud

on the spring forest floor I
squat and I see the sliver
of two front teeth in the mouth's
crescent and the dead silver

down of the ear. A beetle
wends its way through the hair.
When it reaches the raw wound,
stops and begins to feed there.

Winter Wardrobe

Remember that dress I wore?
Raw red silk.
Colour of those poisonous berries
that appear in the fall
on wasted brown stems
and last through the winter.

Sometimes I take your coat out of the closet.
Black tweed one
that smells of every place we went together
when the weather gets cold.
I tie an old belt around it
go out in to the field behind the house.

A single bird.
A flock of birds rises.
A skeletal bush.

I thought they were leftover leaves
that had clung past their season;
but now the bush is bare.

Nothing can outlast
this winter's wind.

I Worry Where I Will Be Buried

I wonder as I ride the Go train
and it hurtles past piles of broken metal,
past crumpled trees in sleeting rain
where black crows wing down to settle,
did anybody ever love this land?
Dream of seeing it thick with grain.

I have seen it fanned
out alongside the train every day.
Imagined its contours intimately known
when it was still farm and field.
Or even farther back when it was overgrown
and nature had yet to yield.

This is why I worry where I will be buried,
for what if it is unloved land to which I'm finally carried.

AGMV Marquis

MEMBER OF THE SCABRINI GROUP

Quebec, Canada
2001